Welsh Football

Editorial & Subscription Address

David Collins,
57 Thornhill Road,
Rhiwbina,
Cardiff CF14 6PE
Telephone: 029 20753179

X: @CollinsWFM
E. Mail: info@welsh-football.net
Website: www.welsh-football.net
: @welshfootballmagazine

Printers:

Harris Printers
18 Mary Street, Porthcawl CF36 3YA
Tel: 01656 788038
nch@harrisprinters.co.uk
www.harrisprinters.co.uk

Cover:
Glyncorrwg FC.

**COPY DEADLINE FOR ISSUE 257
FRIDAY 11th OCTOBER 2024**

*The views expressed in this magazine are not
necessarily those of the editor.*

Contributors:

Stuart Townsend   John Higgins
Jeff Jones   FCHD
FAW Photography

SUBSCRIBE NOW!

Get Welsh Football as soon as it is published and save money.

A new 1 year subscription costs £30 - cheques payable to WELSH FOOTBALL please, and send to:-

Welsh Football, 57 Thornhill Road, Cardiff CF14 6PE (or email us for online payment options)

FRIENDS OF WELSH FOOTBALL

WANTED - any information, especially pictorial, relating to the **history of the game in South Wales** between 1890 and 1900. Please contact Phil Sweet on 0774 989 8986 or email philip.sweet693@btinternet.com

WANTED: Collector and researcher always interested in purchasing old **programmes from Welsh League clubs** in the Swansea area, e.g. Ammanford, Clydach, Pontardawe, Morriston, Grovesend, Skewen, Godrergraig, Atlas Sports, 3M (Gorseinon). Please contact niall_obrien83@hotmail.com

TERRY B: (CARDIFF) Subscriber to Welsh Football Magazine since 1996 - Wouldn't (couldn't) be without it. Huge thanks to David, and others, involved in its continued production. Good luck to Cardiff Draconians FC.

WANTED: Tilbury v Collier Row programme ICIS Lg2 Friday 5.4.96. Also run, sell, swap programmes for **Dartford FC.** Many non-league and some league. Visit us on matchdays in THE POD or send email with wants to barrydartsfc@gmail.com

HIGHADMIT PROJECTS LTD SOUTH WALES PREMIER LEAGUE are proud to support Welsh Football magazine. For full details of the league and its clubs visit our website at www.southwalesallianceleague.co.uk

The **VALE OF GLAMORGAN REFEREES SOCIETY**, sponsored by RIM Motors of Barry. The independent friendly referees society in Wales. Everyone welcome. For meeting dates go to our website www.pitchero.com/clubs/valeofglamorganrefereessociety or contact us at vogrs@hotmail.co.uk.

AMMANFORD AFC/CPD RHYDAMAN - Come down and join the *Black & White Army* at the Recreation Ground this season at Ammanford AFC. If you have any old programmes/pictures/stories/memorabilia about the club, contact: rhodrijones@btconnect.com

CPD PORTHMADOG FC: Home programmes available at £2 each + £1 postage - please contact Dylan - rees48wesla@gmail.com. Visit our online Club Shop: porthmadogfc.com/siop.htm

Copies still available of **TREFEURIG'S YELLOW CANARIES, 1948-1953**: 70 Aberystwyth & District League footballers (2009) and The footballers of Borth & Ynys-las, 1873-1950 (2010), £6 and £5 respectively (post-free) from the author: Richard E. Huws, Pantgwyn, Bont-goch, Ceredigion, SY24 5DP

ALAN DODD (CARMARTHEN): Good luck to all our Welsh teams - more successful campaigns to follow.

CLIFF JONES (NEWPORT) - Welsh football supporter since witnessing Wales qualifying for 1958 World Cup! See you in Cardiff for the World Cup qualifiers !

NEWLANDS PHOTOGRAPHIC are a niche market publisher of books on football grounds and stadia. For full details please email mikefloate55@gmail.com

FOOTBALL - WHEREVER IT MAY BE: don't miss Laurence Reade's essays in words and pictures on groundhopping adventures in England, Wales, Scotland and further afield. Visit laurencereade.com

FREE! Due to programme surplus – Offer 1 mixed bundle English non-league & Welsh programmes; or offer 2 - 20 mixed English non-league; or offer 3 - 20 Welsh programmes. Just send £5 to cover postage & packing. Allan Rushby, 41 Ffordd Ger-y-Llyn, Tircoed, Swansea SA4 9ZJ.

FLOODLIT PITCH-SHINING A LIGHT ON FOOTBALL: Covering football's wonderful grounds, a bit of history, lots of photos, mostly non-league, attempts at humour - you can read it here www.floodlitpitch. blogspot.com

'FROM SAINTS TO DRUIDS – a discovery of Welsh football' an account of travels in the Cymru Premier 2019/20 by Michael Grimes.
Available from https://www.dognduck.net/ or contact michaelbgrimes10@gmail.com

TO ALL FANS OF WELSH FOOTBALL: Enjoy every game! John Longshaw, Warrington.

MARTIN HOARE, CYMRO, BIRMINGHAM: Gwnewch y Pethau Bychain
To all true supporters following all the Welsh non-league clubs, best wishes from the other side of the border, from all at **RAMSBOTTOM UNITED**. Tony Cunningham, Rams Secretary.

Good luck always to **WREXHAM, WALES AND HOLYHEAD HOTSPUR.** Onwards & Upwards and Always Keep the Faith – G.M. Davies

WANTED: NON LEAGUE PAPER I am seeking bulk back copies for a Groundhopper project I am about to commence. I am willing to pay carriage costs, both ways, to anyone who could supply me and wishes papers returned. Contact Stuart Hogg, ten2oneplus@btinternet.com

PUT YOUR CLASSIFIED AD OR MESSAGE ON THIS PAGE! Up to 40 words for just £12 a year As a thank-you to subscribers who pay £12 or more for an advertisement in WFM (or who make similar donations), their magazine subscription will be upgraded to first class postage.

EDITORIAL

Welcome to issue 256 of Welsh Football.

This is our second issue of 2024-25, following issue 255 in August which was the Guide to the new season. This time we have over a month's action to review and so the emphasis of this issue is very different – as much coverage as possible of the various competitions that have started, plus a return to our regular features content alongside that. We have club features and the first of this season's Looking Back series delving into the back story of football in Wales.

Publication of this issue was held back until we knew the outcome of The New Saints' play-off round fixtures in the UEFA Conference League. That was Welsh football history in the making and had to be included in this issue (see pages 16-17).

For the Welsh champions to reach this stage represents a milestone in the story of our national league and there does appear to be widespread recognition of this, and congratulations for TNS, its owner, managers and players. It feels very different to have Welsh interest in European club competition stretching right through until the Christmas period, with TNS involved in six group stage fixtures. It's very good to see Wales removed from the list of European countries never to have been represented beyond the qualifying rounds, and it's not something I was sure I'd ever see.

We'll be covering the group stage campaign in forthcoming issues. The next issue, WF 257, should include news of the first of those, plus Craig Bellamy's first games as Cymru's Nations League fixtures get underway.

I must again thank those renewing subscribers who made donations with their subscription payments. It's thanks to these gestures that I'm able to produce the occasional edition like this one with extra pages and more colour.

Towards the end of September Groundhop UK will run a weekend centred on the Macron West Wales Premier League and I hope to see a number of readers then (weekend of 20-22 September, for details please contact groundhopuk@gmail.com). It's good that this event is still in the calendar after plans to run the traditional August Bank Holiday event in Wales fell through again this year despite the efforts of Groundhop UK. It does appear that this prestigious weekend slot, and the revenue it always generated, have now been lost to grassroots Welsh football.

Dave Collins

Callum Sainty of Barry Town United and Tom Vincent of Cardiff Met, pictured during the south Wales rivals' 1-1 draw at Cyncoed Stadium in August.

Caernarfon Town's Phil Mooney tackles Ben Ahmun of Haverfordwest County in the JD Cymru Premier fixture at the Oval in August. The Bluebirds won 2-1 to continue their promising start to the new campaign.
[photo FAW Photography / Sam Eaden]

Haverfordwest striker Ben Fawcett attempts a shot during his side's 0-0 draw at Cardiff Met on August Bank Holiday Monday, but this effort was too high. The sides were both unbeaten at the start of play and remained so in a game of few chances.

JD CYMRU LEAGUES

We've now had just over a month of action in the Cymru Leagues, beginning with the leagues' Nathaniel MG Cup opening rounds, followed by the first league fixtures. It's still too early to read much into tables or even results.

However, the opening month has brought not only all the early fixtures for all 44 Cymru League members, but significant other news, with some prominent managers parting ways with their clubs in August.

Neil Gibson's departure from Connah's Quay Nomads took just about everyone by surprise, and no real explanation has been given. Gibson's side had, after all, finished second in the Cymru Premier last season, and although they had already been eliminated from both the UEFA Conference League and the Nathaniel MG Cup, there wasn't any indication of a crisis.

Billy Paynter was quite quickly appointed after a selection process. A very experienced EFL player, he has held several coaching and management positions, most recently at Runcorn Linnets. It's an interesting appointment of someone not well-known in Cymru League circles.

At the other end of the country, the departure of Gruff Harrison from Ammanford was also surprising, not least for its timing in the opening week of the league season. But it appears simply to be a personal decision after twelve demanding years, during which Harrison had overseen the west Walians' rise from the Welsh League's lower divisions to become a respected second-tier outfit. Both he and the club highlighted his legacy, and an orderly transition is expected, as Harrison has been succeeded by Wyn Thomas. Already part of the management team at the Rec., the former Aberystwyth, Carmarthen, Haverfordwest and Llanelli player brings a wealth of Cymru Premier experience to the club.

Meanwhile, in the Cymru North, Matty Roberts resigned at Prestatyn Town three games into the season – his side having suffered a couple of heavy defeats. Roberts had been at Bastion Gardens for just over six months, but had saved the Seasiders from relegation into tier 3. Some stability is badly needed.

Turning now to the news of action on the field, the Cymru Premier got off to a slightly disrupted start with TNS still involved in Europe, and league games sensibly postponed to allow them the best preparations possible. Every win or draw in TNS's European campaign is so clearly in the league's best interests, so it was disappointing to read criticism of this 'concession' from some within the league, though we expected it from the predictable keyboard warriors who only ever post negatively about the Welsh champions.

It did, however, create an opportunity for rivals to steal a march on the champions, and the south Wales trio of Penybont, Haverfordwest and Cardiff Met were all unbeaten in the opening four rounds of games. TNS will have to play catch up but, given the depth of Craig Harrison's squad, their extended European adventure shouldn't be too much of an issue.

The newcomers have as expected found life in the top flight tough, with Briton Ferry in particular conceding goals at an alarming rate. We can't write anyone off yet, but finding their feet in the autumn will be crucial for Ferry and Flint.

In the second tier, Airbus UK made a perfect start, reeling off six straight wins to open up an early lead. They meet relegated Colwyn Bay in September, and champions Holywell in October, games which all the chasing pack hope will lower the Wingmakers' colours.

After six rounds, the picture in the Cymru South is a little different. It's a promoted side, Ttethomas Bluebirds, who have been making the early season headlines here winning their opening four before being held to draws by Trefelin and Caerau Ely.

Trefelin are also among the teams impressing in the opening weeks, with the seemingly evergreen Lee Trundle prominent after surprisingly stepping up from tier 3. The Swansea idol, 48 next month, missed much of last season with a serious injury but has bounced back with five league goals already for Trefelin.

Newport City, promoted from the Ardal South East with Trethomas this summer, have also made a positive start to life in tier 2, with wins over Ammanford, Caerau Ely and Penrhiwceiber Rangers in the first month of the season.

Above left: Llantwit Major players celebrate a goal by Nathan Renfree as they begin the season with a 2-0 Nathaniel MG Cup win over fellow Cymru South side Newport City. That was as far as the Major would go in the competition, as they were knocked out by Cardiff Met in the next round.

Above right: Mid Wales rivals Penrhyncoch and Guilsfield met in the Nathaniel MG Cup opening round with the Guils coming away from Ceredigion with a comfortable 0-3 victory. Guilsfield went on to draw 2-2 at Llandudno in the second round, but lost on penalties.
[photo Stuart Townsend]

Left: Craig Lindfield gives Colwyn Bay a one goal lead in the eagerly anticipated derby clash at Llandudno in the JD Cymru North. A late equaliser by substitute Lee Stokes meant the north Wales coast neighbours had to share the points.
[photo FAW Photography / Sam Eaden]

Bottom left: Gresford Athletic came from 2-0 down to pull off a 2-4 win over Penrhyncoch in the JD Cymru North, with five of the six goals coming in a hectic first half at Cae Baker.
[photo FAW Photography / Lewis Mitchell]

TAFF'S WELL REMEMBER NORMA SAMUEL

On Friday 12ᵗʰ July 2024 Taffs Well welcomed Merthyr Town to their Gentles Construction Stadium in the inaugural Norma Samuel Memorial Cup. I went along with my twin brother Stephen and his son Leigh both Merthyr Town followers. I was supporting the Wellmen (see picture) in view of my years as committee man and match programme editor there.

Norma who served not only the Wellmen as secretary since 1996 was also a member of the Welsh League committee. Norma sadly left us in January this year and in June her Husband Steve who is also the Taffs Well grounds man picked up a special award at the FAW National League awards in honour of her great contribution to football.

At the time of her passing Merthyr Town had issued public recognition of the sadness they felt and thanks for the part Norma (and Don James) had played in keeping the Martyrs alive by allowing the "new" club to rent the ground at Taffs Well, having been prevented from playing at their Penydarren home after Merthyr Tydfil FC had gone bankrupt.

Merthyr then were the obvious opponents on a night that started with a minute's applause. It was also fitting that the visitors chose a red and green kit as they were the colours they wore during their two season in exile at Taffs.

The hosts had gone to a lot of trouble in preparation for the game and there was fast food available as well as a printed match programmes. The crowd number then was a tad disappointing 223, this the week before the two sides were to meet in the first round of the Nathaniel MG Cup.

The visitors proved too strong for the Wellmen on the night winning the game 6-1 with goals from Kane Williams who hit a hat-trick and others from Cawley Cox, Liam Angel and Jac Clay. Sam Johnson got the hosts' consolation goal.

At the end of the match Steve Samuel presented the Merthyr captain with the silverware. The game will be an annual event and is a fitting and lasting tribute to Norma Samuel who was a great servant to both Taffs Well and the game at amateur level in Wales.

Jeff Jones

Photos: below left, the Jones twins. Below right, the memorial game underway with the trophy in the foreground.

Over 200 clubs set out on the Welsh Cup trail in late July, with the First Qualifying Round bringing a predictable mix of high-scoring ties and close ones, surprises, penalty shoot-outs and a few withdrawals to boot.

In the northern half of the draw, Ardal League Bow Street came unstuck in a surprise defeat at Cemaes Bay, and Sychdyn United almost pulled off another shock, only losing to Llanberis on penalties. Meanwhile in the south, Cwrt Rawlin from tier 6 drew 3-3 at Ardal League South Gower and then won the shoot-out, while Holton Road (also tier 6) did even better, winning 3-0 over Ardal club Bridgend Street.

Photos on this page:

Top: Clydach FC striker Nathan Jones races clear before beating the Tregaron Turfs keeper for his side's third goal in an 8-3 win at Coed Gwilym Park.

Middle: Another Central Wales League side, Carno, caused one of the upsets of the first qualifying round when they defeated Radnor Valley of the Ardal NE 2-1 at Tŷ Brith. Ioan Humphreys and Josh Matthews scored the goals.

Bottom: Tier 5 Llangoed & District hosted a local Anglesey derby with comparative giants Llangefni Town, the visitors coming out on top with a 0-4 win at Tyddyn Paun.

[photo FAW Photography / Sam Eaden]

The survivors from the First Qualifying Round went on to play in the Second Qualifying Round, hoping to reach the competition proper in September when the Cymru North and South clubs enter.

With this year's draws being split only into north and south regions, there were again some interesting pairings with clubs able to meet unfamiliar opposition rather than their regular local league adversaries. Let's hope this format of draw is maintained in future.

Highlights of the round included a huge 13-0 win for St Joseph's and a surprise 3-4 victory for Aber Valley over Pontardawe Town, while up north Gaerwen pulled off a shock 2-0 win at Rhos Aelwyd.

Photos on this page:

Top: Cardiff Corries's Mo Abdullah sees his touch send the ball past Blaenavon keeper Elliot Matthews for his side's third goal in a 4-1 victory at the Blues' Memorial Ground in the Second Qualifying Round.

Middle: CPD Llanberis hosted Bontnewydd at scenic Ffordd Padarn, the home side prevailing 4-1.

photo FAW Photography / John Smith]

Bottom: Penmaenmawr Phoenix (in yellow and blue) met Pwllheli at Cae Sling, overlooking the Menai Strait, and the NWCFA West League side scored a memorable 5-2 win over their tier 3 visitors.

[photo FAW Photography / Sam Eaden]

12

ARDAL LEAGUES (TIER 3)

The Ardal Leagues were among the early starters in Wales so we have had a few matchdays to see which clubs are exceeding, meeting or falling short of expectations so far.

Porthmadog is one example of a club doing nicely in its bid to make a quick return to tier 2. Then came the bombshell of Chris Jones and assistant Mark Seddon resigning in mid-August. Jones was soon unveiled as the new boss at Runcorn Town in the North West Counties League over the border... BUT then a week later Jones and Seddon were back at the Traeth.

Port' started the season as one of the obvious favourites and a 5-2 win over NFA during the management team's week away kept them on track. The disruption had looked likely to be a setback in the promotion bid, but with the swift return to the status quo that's less of a worry.

The Ardal Leagues are proving fascinating divisions with so many membership changes year on year – eighteen new clubs arriving from above and below each season, and others switching between the four divisions to even up the numbers. So clubs tend to face plenty of unfamiliar opponents every season.

Predicting how the newcomers will fare is no easy job. Among this year's crop coming up from the tier 4 leagues, there have been notably strong starts in the Ardal North East for Kerry (promoted from the Central Wales North) and in the Ardal North West for Connah's Quay Town (who came up from the North East Wales League) and Trearddur Bay (from the North Wales Coast West). But on the other hand Menai Bridge Tigers had a tough start, losing their first four Ardal North West fixtures.

In the Ardal Southern Leagues Evans & Williams from Llanelli made the best start of all the newcomers, , sitting second in the table at the end of August after half a dozen games in the South West division.

Another notable feature of the first month has been the early form of the Cardiff clubs in the Ardal Southern Leagues. Canton FC have made a fine start in the Ardal SE after being moved laterally from the SW division, their early results including wins over Chepstow Town and Abertillery Bluebirds, who had both enjoyed positive starts of their own.

Cardiff Corinthians and Cardiff Draconians were both unbeaten and among the early leaders of the South West division at the end of August, these two having met already and shared the points in the opening weeks. But aless comfortable opening month for fellow capital city outfit Bridgend Street, promoted from the South Wales Alliance in the summer, though they did get off the mark at the end of July with a somewhat unexpected win over Cefn Cribwr.

Clearly there is a long way to go in all these divisions, and after the busy initial month of fixtures, cup commitments will dominate for a few weeks, with many clubs still involved in the Welsh Cup, FAW Amateur Trophy and of course the two Ardal League Cup competitions, whose first rounds are scheduled for late August, just after we go to press.

Top left: Bridgend Street made their Ardal SW debut in a home derby against city rivals Cardiff Corries, but it was a night to forget as the visitors (in the grey kit) came away with a convincing 2-6 victory.

Top right: Morriston Town keeper Steve Cann saves a penalty from Cardiff Dracs' Sam Cawley, but his side still went down to a 1-0 defeat at Lydstep Park in the Ardal SW in early August.

Middle row: Newport Corinthians in blue celebrate their first home goal in the Ardal SE at upgraded Coronation Park, equalising a first half strike by visitors Croesyceiliog. In the end, the two sides, both promoted from the Gwent Premier League, had to settle for a point apiece as Croesyceiliog grabbed a last minute goal to level at 2-2.

Bottom row: Abergavenny Town and Canton could not be separated as they met at the Pen-y-Pound Stadium on the opening night of the Floodlighting and Electrical Ardal South East. The hosts featured a number of new signings amongst their ranks, following their relegation from JD Cymru South, but were unable to find a way past a well-organised defence.

[photo Stuart Townsend]

Top: Radnor Valley claimed a dramatic stoppage time goal courtesy of Matt Croose to draw 2-2 with hosts Llandrindod Wells on Wednesday 31st July in their Lock Stock Ardal North East Radnorshire derby on The Broadway.
[photo Stuart Townsend]

Middle: Undy have had a mixed start to the new season, suffering two heavy defeats in July, but salvaged a point with a stoppage time equaliser in this all-Gwent Ardal SE clash at Plough Road, Goytre, which finished 2-2.
[photo Stuart Townsend]

Bottom: With the town's annual jazz festival being a backdrop to proceedings, Brecon Corinthians hit all the right notes on Saturday 10th August, as they defeated Caldicot Town 4-1 at the Rich Field to move into second position in the Ardal South East table.
[photo Stuart Townsend]

HISTORIC MOMENT FOR TNS & WALES

Over recent years we've tended to bemoan the bad luck in UEFA Draws suffered by Cymru Premier clubs, especially in the Champions League. But this year has been different: and thankfully Welsh champions TNS have taken advantage of the opportunities presented to them and have finally broken through into a European competition's 'group stage'.

In the last issue, we reported on the Saints win over Decic in the first qualifying round of Champions League, and already knew that Hungarian champions Ferencváros would probably be too strong for any further progress in the flagship UEFA competition.

But, as we noted then, UEFA's competition formats are forgiving for champions clubs. This recognises that champions of smaller nations were badly disadvantaged by allowing non-champions from the top nations into the Champions League. The 'consolation' is a second chance after elimination from the Champions League, in the Europa League; and indeed a third chance after that, in the Conference League.

After losing home and away to Ferencváros, TNS faced Petrocub of Moldova in the Europa League, knowing that an aggregate win would guarantee qualification for a group stage. Hopes were high, but disappointingly TNS failed to score in either leg and were edged out 1-0 on aggregate.

So that left one last chance, and again there could be no complaints about the draw: Lithuanian champions Panevėžys had a similar path to the Conference League Play-Off Round, dropping down after exiting the two other competitions, but crucially their domestic form was known to be poor – a stroke of luck.

Once again hopes were high, and on this occasion the first leg in Vilnius on 22nd August brought a dominant, professional performance by Craig Harrison's men, establishing a 3-0 lead to take back to Park Hall, thanks to goals from Danny Davies, Danny Williams and Ben Clark.

Back at Park Hall for the second leg on 29th August, Craig Harrison clearly wasn't taking any risks. His side gave a disciplined, but mostly cautious, performance to ensure the first leg advantage wasn't squandered, and it was preserved by a 0-0 draw on the night. Less excitement, but this was a night so important, historically, that the outcome had to take priority.

At the final whistle, there was relief, then celebration. The stadium loudspeaker played "Dancing in the Streets of TNS" and the players posed for the cameras with a Welsh flag.

Less than 24 hours later came the group stage draw in Monaco, when TNS discovered that their fixture schedule will take them to Florence to play Fiorentina, Dublin to face Shamrock Rovers and Slovenia to play Celje, while they'll host Djurgarden, Panathinaikos and Astana.

Our champions clubs have been competing in Europe for over 30 years and getting into the competition 'proper' of one of the tournaments has been regarded as the Holy Grail. TNS owner Mike Harris has talked of it as his goal for years. The past hasn't even really brought any near misses, but the introduction of the Conference League as UEFA's third competition has certainly put it in reach, provided everything falls into place. TNS have built up a ranking over the years that increases their chances of seeding, but even so the luck of the draw is key. This year the stars aligned and, thankfully, the opportunity was taken.

The Welsh champions' progress will mean several things. Most obviously, it gives them six high-profile fixtures between October and December (see the supplement for details). And they will earn serious levels of prize money for their participation, with further financial opportunities through sponsorship, TV rights etc.

But it's not just the champions themselves who benefit. There are solidarity payments to the FAW for clubs who don't qualify for Europe, but even more significantly every win or draw that TNS achieve in any of the three competitions counts as co-efficient points that affect Wales's ranking. Already TNS's efforts seem to have done enough to restore our fourth place in Europe in 2026.

For various reasons, The New Saints have long been a somewhat divisive subject. But there's no denying the contribution they have made to our reputation and standing in Europe. However hard some people find it, we really should all be celebrating their achievements this summer.

Above: Ryan Brobbel takes the ball forward for TNS in their UEFA Champions League fixture with Hungarian champions Ferencváros at Park Hall on 30th July.

Middle row, left: Adam Wilson in action against Panevėžys at Park Hall.

Middle row, right: Leo Smith delivers a corner.

Bottom row, left: Sion Bradley makes a late substitute appearance.

Bottom row, right: TNS celebrate qualification for the UEFA Conference Group Stage, after the final whistle at Park Hall on 29th August [this image by FAW Photography].

The Dragon Signs FAW Amateur Trophy again attracted a bumper entry, with clubs from over 30 different leagues all participating, from the third-tier Ardal Leagues to local district leagues. Numbers allowed for almost everyone to be involved in the Qualifying round fixtures on the first weekend of August, and there were inevitably some big scores and also a few surprises.

Top scorers were Kerry, who put twelve goals past Central Wales League opponents Penybont United, with Seaside of Llanelli also getting double figures, against Gower side Penclawdd of the Swansea Senior League.

Swansea also produced a couple of more unexpected results, with local league side Blaenymaes eliminating Swansea University (Ardal SW) and Mumbles Rangers defeating Clydach FC.

In the northern section, Cemaes Bay's 5-1 win over Ardal League outfit NFA was a surprise, and another Ardal League side, Llangefni Town, lost an Anglesey derby to CPD Boded. Bethesda Rovers also unexpectedly claimed a place in the First Round with a win on penalties after holding Llandudno Junction to a 3-3 draw.

On these pages we bring action from just a few of the Qualifying Round ties. The First Round proper takes place in September and we'll have further coverage in WF 257.

Abergavenny Town, newly relegated from tier 2, got their first win of the new season at the third attempt, beating Tredegar Town 2-1 in the first qualifying round of the Dragon Signs FAW Amateur Trophy at the Pen-y-Pound Stadium. Town had lost in the Welsh Cup a week earlier and been held at home by Risca in the league opener, but a penalty from Mason Keepin-Davies (pictured) and a second goal from Rudi Griffiths saw them through to the First Round.
[photo Stuart Townsend]

Clydach Wasps bounced back from trailing 0-2 at half-time to defeat Autocentre Gwent Premier League Premier Division rivals Newport Saints FC 5-3 on penalties in the Dragon Signs FAW Amateur Trophy first qualifying round at the Clydach Recreation Ground. [photo Stuart Townsend]. The Saints led thanks to long-range efforts from Jay Saunders and Ellis McLoughlin but couldn't hold on as Ben Sherman drew the sides level, and it was Wasps keeper Ellis Owens who was the shoot-out hero.

GLYNCORRWG F.C. °

Among another bumper entry for the Dragon Signs FAW Amateur Trophy was Glyncorrwg AFC, currently of the Port Talbot & District League. Their fixture immediately caught my interest, because the village of Glyncorrwg is one with a half-forgotten Welsh League past.

Glyncorrwg joined fellow Afan valley club Gwynfi United in the Welsh League in the early 1930s, but unlike their near neighbours, do not appear to have climbed the league's divisions during a spell that spanned the second world war. After finishing in the lower reaches of Division 2 (West) once again in 1950-51, Glyncorrwg left the league but returned in 1954, finally achieving a top-half place in Div 2 (W) in 1959-60 (fourth behind Carmarthen, Clydach and Pontardawe. Fifth a year later, fortunes declined again from 1961, but the club remained as league strugglers until 1969-70.

For the past half century, Glyncorrwg (also sometimes Glyncorrwg United) have mostly played district league football, punctuated by periods of abeyance, but with a two-season spell in the old South Wales Senior League from 2000 to 2002. Under the name Glyncorrwg Hall, the village club won the SWFA Intermediate Cup in 2006 and 2007. The most recent revival has resulted in promotion to the Port Talbot League's higher division and it was pleasing to see the club enter this season's FAW Trophy.

A draw against Ardal South West opposition South Gower could have meant a tough debut in the national competition but Glyncorrwg battled hard after going 0-2 down to the visitors in the opening quarter hour. When Scott Pearce pulled a goal back before half time hopes of a comeback were raised, but the tier 3 visitors clung on, netting a late goal for a 1-3 win.

Glyncorrwg is a former mining village in the scenic valley of the Nant Corrwg, a tributary of the river Afan. The village's football ground is Ynyscorrwg Park, just south of the village close to walking and biking trails. An infrequent bus serves the village from Port Talbot, but a good option on a fine day is to catch the more frequent bus from Bridgend to Cymmer, and walk along the riverside path that follows the track-bed of a former railway line, through splendid scenery.

Photos: South Gower winger Koki Izumi in action in the Trophy match at Glyncorrwg, and below a panorama of the scenic Ynyscorrwg Park venue.

19

PROGRAMME NOTES

Regular readers will know that printed programmes have become less common since the pandemic, much to the chagrin of programme afficionados and collectors. With each new season, there has almost been an expectation that the situation will be worse, with more clubs going down the dreaded 'online issue' route. But my impressions over the last couple of months have been different – a healthy flow – well, trickle – of domestic issues has already arrived here for review.

Those will have to wait, as this month I'm looking at the printed programmes issued for the UEFA club games involving TNS, Nomads, Caernarfon and Bala. And here too, the reality has been considerably better than some of us anticipated ahead of the qualifying round games.

THE NEW SAINTS have tended to be reliable issuers in Europe and once again a typically professional programme has been produced for each of their home ties to date. These are smart, informative 48-page colour issues produced for the club by JJ Sports Promotions, and they create exactly the sort of impression that you'd hope for from the champions of Wales.

CONNAH'S QUAY NOMADS did also issue for the visit of NK Bravo in the Europe League, a smart 32-page production on stiff card stock, with the content weighted towards photos rather than words. Again, a thoroughly acceptable souvenir issue for a European tie.

BALA TOWN hadn't been expected to issue, so for anything to be available at Park Hall for the tie v Paide was a pleasant surprise, although to be honest the production, print quality and amount of content wasn't a patch on the two mentioned above.

CAERNARFON TOWN said they didn't have the resources to issue, although they did compile an online version. Some copies of this got printed, but not officially as far as I am aware.

As for the away games, even avid collectors often don't know when and where to expect a programme of any sort. Sometimes they aren't available to all spectators – only VIPs etc – and then again there's the pitfall of 'pirate' programmes masquerading as official issues, just produced for the Ebay market to exploit collectors.

But the CRUSADERS v Caernarfon issue was real enough, another 32-page production on stiff card, with a good balance of content and photos. PAIDE produced a more modest 8-page programme, but crucially it didn't cost the £3 that those above were charging - it was probably free.

For FERENCVAROS v TNS, the Hungarian club produced a very professional 28-page issue (looking like a regular issue) containing a nice 2-page feature on the Welsh champions.

In summary, a respectable haul of print issues from this season's UEFA games (and potentially more to come). My thanks go to those readers who helped me to assemble this collection for review.

Dave Collins

AROUND THE REGIONS

Having issued our Guide to 2024-25 back at the end of July, it was inevitable that there would be changes to the competitions previewed before the action really started.

The most obvious change came in mid Wales, where we lost one league altogether from the pyramid chart published in the Guide. It wasn't a complete shock that the revival of the Mid Wales League (South) at tier 5 didn't get off the ground. The league had been in abeyance in 2023-24, with its clubs joining the Montgomeryshire League, or crossing the border to Gwent and SWFA-controlled leagues. Even the return of reserve teams to local football couldn't boost the numbers enough to make for a viable league, especially as Talgarth Town resisted the CWFA's attempt to force them to return from the Gwent Central League.

Elsewhere, a few leagues and divisions saw late changes to membership. In WF 255 we referred to an issue affecting the South Wales Premier League, where either Bettws or Cardiff Bay Warriors were expected to be placed on promotion to the tier 5 Championship division, but which of them was the subject of protracted arbitration. In the end the saga was resolved with both clubs playing in an enlarged division, leaving odd numbers in two of the SWPL's four sections.

One late addition to the North East Wales League was notable because it concerned such a famous name: Cefn Druids. Returning to football after disappearing ignominiously from tier 2 in 2023, the Druids club was added into the tier 5 Championship division along with the area's recreational outfits. Druids returned to action on 17th August in an away fixture at Bellevue, famously a club where participation and inclusivity are the priorities, and where points have often been hard to come by. And rather as expected, Druids raced into a two goal half time lead, but then saw Bellevue rally in the second half to earn a memorable 2-2 draw.

In fact, the North East Wales League saw as many new clubs this summer as any competition, but fortunes have been predictably mixed. Broughton United have hit the ground running, sitting as early leaders of the tier 5 Championship Division in late August, whereas others like CPD Cei Connah, Deeside United and Deeside Dragons have found things a lot tougher – especially the Dragons, who've been on the wrong end of the sort of big scores usually associated with Bellevue. At least the league membership still stood at its planned 16 after a month of the season, contrary to some predictions.

Withdrawals before a ball was kicked included Gwent tier 4 club Cwmffrwdoer Sports and 5 side Neuadd Wen. Cwmffrwdoer cited a lack of management and players when quitting the league in mid August, but they remain in the Gwent Central League, with the second eleven now becoming the firsts by default. This Pontypool-based club similarly disappeared from the Gwent League in 2017, returning via promotion from the Gwent Central after the pandemic.

The earliest competitive action for grassroots clubs was in the national cups (covered separately in this issue, see pages 10-11 and 18-19). And, as always, the start of the season was far from uniform around the country, with a few leagues going for early August, to complete some rounds of games before the weather intervenes, but many left it much later. Pembrokeshire and Cardiff parks leagues are traditionally late, with playing fields and some players still committed to cricket.

The Gwent region began the season with some local cup action, with two rounds of the Gwent Premier's County Motors Challenge Cup completed in August, leaving only 16 teams standing. Quite a few of the league's Premier Division sides fell by the wayside, some by other Premier Division opposition, but Cwmbran Town were beaten by Marshfield and Lucas Cwmbran by Mardy.

The Central Wales League's North and South divisions both managed to fit in several rounds of matches before August was out, with newcomers Ffostrasol racing to the top of the South division with four straight wins By contrast, it was the bigger, more established names who dominated the early rounds in the North division, with Welshpool Town, Llanrhaeadr and Carno all unbeaten in the early weeks.

Below the Central Wales League the Ceredigion League played several rounds of fixtures in August, and last season's runners-up Felinfach were the only side to make it through the month with a 100 percent record – maybe not such a surprise considering they finished only five points behind the strong Ffostrasol side last season.

Another league in full swing during August was the Macron West Wales Premier League, now running with a full complement of 16 clubs. The early signs here are of possible domination by the league's powerful Swansea clubs, with former champions Penlan and Rockspur now joined by St. Joseph's, who came up as Swansea Senior League champions. Scoring 21 goals in the opening four fixtures, the Saints made their mark immediately and are clearly going to be a force. Alongside the Swansea sides, Pontarddulais Town showed good early form that is in marked contrast to their results in recent seasons, and appear to be a different proposition this season. Cwmamman United, now in their second season in this league after relegation from the Ardal South West, also appear potential contenders, having already taken points from Penlan (a 5-3 win) and St. Joseph's (the first side to avoid defeat against the newcomers).

Further east, there has been a little less league action during August, so it's too early to draw any conclusions. However, it's worth noting several clubs promoted from district leagues into tier 6 who made really positive starts aafter this big step up: In Gwent, Alway won their first two games in the Gwent Premier's tier 6 division, while Splott Cons, Talbot Green and Caerau All Whites all boasted similar records two rounds into the South Wales Premier Division One season (again a tier 6 league).

First photo: Knighton Town came out on top in the Radnorshire derby on Tuesday 6th August when they defeated a spirited Penybont United 7-1 in the Central Wales League (South) at Bryn-y-Castell [photo by Stuart Townsend]. The Robins have proved to be among the early pace-setters in this division, with four straight wins during August.

Second photo: Macron West Wales Premier League action as league newcomers St. Joseph's record a convincing 8-0 win over Garden Village on the new 3G surface at Underhill Park, Mumbles. Darren Griffiths is pictured seizing on a rebound to open the scoring, and he went on to complete a rapid first half hat-trick, ending the game with four of his side's goals.

Above: North East Wales league newcomers Broughton United have made a strong start to their debut season and are pictured In the amber shirts during a 2-1 win over Brymbo at their home pitch in Saltney Ferry.
[photo by John Higgins]

Middle photo: Also in the North East Wales League Division One, CPD Yr Wyddgrug have moved from their former base at the Northop Hall pavilion, to the village of Gwernymynydd. This picture, by John Higgins, shows them winning 5-1 at home v Overton Recreation (Yr Wyddgrug in yellow and black).

Bottom photo: Hay St Mary's are back in the Central Wales League (South) following relegation from the Ardal South East and opened their 2024-25 campaign on Wednesday 7th August with a 3-2 win over border rivals Presteigne St.Andrews at Forest Road.
[photo by Stuart Townsend]

23

WOMEN'S FOOTBALL

The domestic women's football season still hasn't really got underway as this second edition of 2024-25 goes to press. League complements are generally smaller in the women's game, but surely it might still be better to take advantage of the late summer weather, et the season started and plan a break in mid-winter?

The Adran Premier and tier 2 Adran Leagues are scheduled to begin in mid-September, after the Adran Trophy has started the season off at the beginning of the month. But that's a full six weeks later than the opening fixtures of the men's season. And the frustrating thing is that it means our European representatives (Cardiff City Women) will not have had competitive domestic action before their UEFA Women's Champions League games in the first week of September. Surely this needs a re-think before next year?

Anyway, while we have been waiting for the season to start, we've already lost a club from the Genero Adran Leagues: Pontardawe Town decided to withdraw from the Adran South, which will unfortunately run with just seven members again this season. Pontardawe had struggled last season, finishing bottom, but had been spared relegation because the league was under complement last term as well – following Abergavenny's demise and Coed Duon's withdrawal mid-season.

Perhaps withdrawals like this, at relatively high level in the pyramid, only serve to illustrate that the female game is still in the process of maturing. Nevertheless, it's a shame that the second-tier clubs in the south will again only play twelve league fixtures all season. The Adran Trophy, however, will have Cambrian United filling the spare slot, the Rhondda club having been handed a wild-card entry to the tier 1 and 2 league cup tournament.

Another symptom of the early stage of development of the women's game is the difficulty we sometimes encounter sourcing even basic information – things like late entry of competitions and fixtures on Comet/Cymru Football, and failure to respond to requests for information. For those of us striving to ensure women's football in Wales gets a respectable level of coverage, it can be rather frustrating, though.

Turning now to the Cymru national team, it's been quiet on this front too - but October will bring the vital UEFA Women's EURO 2025 play-off fixtures against Slovakia – Rhian Wilkinson's side playing the first leg away in Poprad on 25th October, before hosting the second leg in Cardiff four days later on 39th October. Excitement will be building for this during September – and we will finally get to see some competitive domestic action too.

Adran Premier 1st PHASE Fixtures 2024-2025	Aberystwyth	Barry	Briton Ferry	Cardiff C.	Cardiff Met	Swansea C	TNS	Wrexham
Aberystwyth Town		05/01	15/09	27/10	15/12	26/01	03/11	06/10
Barry Town United	29/09		01/12	26/01	19/01	24/11	15/09	13/10
Briton Ferry Llansawel	24/11	02/02		15/12	29/09	27/10	19/01	22/09
Cardiff City	02/02	03/11	13/10		22/09	19/01	29/09	01/12
Cardiff Met University	13/10	06/10	26/01	24/11		15/09	01/12	05/01
Swansea City	01/12	22/09	05/01	06/10	03/11		13/10	02/02
The New Saints	22/09	27/10	06/10	05/01	02/02	15/12		24/11
Wrexham	19/01	15/12	03/11	15/09	27/10	29/09	26/01	

SPOTLIGHT ON CARNO F.C.

Carno Football Club will be celebrating its 65th anniversary next year and therefore it is an apposite time to look back on the club's history. The Montgomeryshire outfit was last featured in this publication in late 2008 when they were plying their trade in the Mid Wales League after having been founder members of the Cymru Alliance in 1990. The Tŷ Brith club have experienced many high and lows over the course of their history, which initially started in the Montgomeryshire League, before eventually progressing into senior football during the early 1980s. Carno's halcyon period was during the early 1990s when they reached the second tier of the domestic pyramid and also faced Wrexham in a Welsh Cup tie at The Racecourse.

The village of Carno lies almost at the watershed between the Severn and Dovey river basins, the meetings point of Welsh and Anglicised cultures, and astride what was the old Roman Road (now the main north-south route through Wales) between the forts at Caersws and Pennal, near Aberdovey. A Roman fort named Gaer Noddfa is located next to the churchyard on the bank of the Afon Carno. A large mound occupies part of the fort and pottery found nearby indicates medieval usage but suggestions that it was a Norman fortification have been rejected. In 952, Iago and Ieuaf, the two exiled sons of Idwal Foel, King of Gwynedd, invaded Dyfed but were defeated in a decisive battle near Carno by the sons of Hywell Dda, King of Deheubarth, and victory secured the sovereignty of north Wales. Carno is renowned as being the burial place of Laura Ashley and where she opened a factory in 1967. The village's name is supposedly derived from the Welsh word for cairn (carnedd) as there are many ancient cairns on the hills surrounding the village.

The idea of establishing a football club occurred after three local men - Bernard Evans, Edward Glyn Jones and Meirion Rowlands - were convalescing in a local public house following a car crash. When the trio recovered, they decided to proceed and took the initial steps to create Carno Football Club, with the first away match played at Llandinam. The players took the train from the village to Moat Lane, but because there was no connection to Llandinam, they had to walk the remainder of the journey. Carno joined the Montgomeryshire League for the 1960/61 season, when they finished twelfth out of 17 teams, and took a number of years to settle into competitive football. The Greens claimed their first title in 1966/67, after finishing two points ahead of Kerry, but I have not able to locate a league table for the following term.

By the 1968/69 season, the Tŷ Brith club had slipped to a lower-half finish and were placed in the newly-formed Second Division for the following campaign. Although the Greens had finished runners-up at the conclusion of their first term in the lower tier, the club were not promoted that season, before going on to conclude the next campaign in sixth position. Carno were promoted to the First Division, but made an instant return, being relegated following the 1971/72 season, and remained for four seasons. The Tŷ Brith outfit secured the Second Division championship in 1975/76, by virtue of finishing a single point ahead of Trewern United, but once again endured demotion 12 months later.

Carno bounced back to secure the Second Division title in 1977/78 before finishing in third position upon their return to the top section. The Greens consolidated their place over the course of the next three seasons before making the decision to move into senior football for the first time in their history. The villagers concluded their debut campaign in fourth position in the Mid Wales League Second Division but had the consolation of lifting the Montgomeryshire Challenge Cup for the first time. Carno were held to a goalless draw by former Montgomeryshire League rivals Llansantffraid before lifting the trophy with a decisive extra-time goal. The league reverted to a single section for the 1983/84 season, with the Ty Brith men finishing in the lower reaches, prior to finishing bottom of the table at the conclusion of the following term.

The Greens returned to the Montgomeryshire League for the 1985/86 season, taking the place of their reserve team in the Second Division, and gained promotion at the first attempt. *[continued overleaf]*

The village club finished runners-up in the Montgomeryshire First Division over the next two seasons, behind Llansantffraid and Berriew respectively, before making their return to senior football for the 1988/89 campaign. Carno finished in the lower echelons at the conclusion of their first season back in the Mid Wales League. A mid-table finish at the end of the following term, allied to the facilities at Ty Brith, saw the Montgomeryshire club invited to become inaugural members of the Cymru Alliance for the 1990/91 season.

Although Carno struggled initially at the higher level, during their first two seasons in the new league, they concluded the 1992/93 campaign in sixth position after several clubs joined the newly-formed League of Wales. This was to be the Greens' highest finish in the domestic pyramid and a considerable achievement for a club that was playing in the Second Division of the Montgomeryshire League only seven seasons earlier. The Tŷ Brithoutfit were unable to repeat their success the following term, as they finished mid-table, but equalled their highest final placing at the conclusion of the 1994/95 season. Unfortunately, for the Montgomeryshire club, the following term saw Gareth Griffiths' charges rooted to the basement of the table, which relegated Carno following six seasons in the Cymru Alliance.

Whilst the Greens finished third upon their return to the Mid Wales League, behind the reserves of Caersws and Newtown, they had the consolation of lifting the League Cup after defeating Penparcau 2-0 in the final. The Tŷ Brith outfit repeated their third-placed finish 12 months later before going down to Caersws in the Montgomeryshire Challenge Cup final during the following term. Carno were finally crowned Mid Wales League champions at the conclusion of the 1999/00 season after finishing four points ahead of former Cymru Alliance rivals Penrhyncoch. The Greens were unable to defend their crown, when the following term was prematurely curtailed by the foot and mouth outbreak, but they were runners-up to the Cae Baker club in 2001/02, four points behind the Roosters, despite scoring a century of league goals; one of only three teams that season to achieve the feat in domestic football.

Mid-table finishes ensued during the flowing three campaigns, although Carno reached the Montgomeryshire Challenge Cup final during the 2002/03 season, when they were once again defeated by the Bluebirds. The following two campaigns resulted in a sharp decline in fortunes, as the Greens finished bottom of the table at the conclusion of the 2005/06 season, and only the presence of Llanidloes Town prevented a repeat performance 12 months later. Manager John Davies, a former Caersws player, brought several new players to Ty Brith during the summer of 2007 to bolster the squad. The club also introduced a reserve team for the first time since 1985 following the introduction of the 'one player, one club' rule by the FAW and entered the Montgomeryshire League Second Division. That season saw the first team ensconced in the safety of mid-table and overcome Cymru Alliance club Guilsfield 5-0 to lift the Montgomeryshire Challenge Cup for only the second time in their history.

The Greens remained in the top-four of the Mid Wales League over the following three seasons and reached another Montgomeryshire Challenge Cup final in 2010/11. However, on this occasion the Ty Brith club suffered a narrow 1-0 reverse at the hands of Montgomery Town.

Pictured right, the Carno team which defeated Guilsfield to win the Central Wales Challenge Cup final in 2015-16.

– THE GREENS

A final day reverse to local rivals Llanidloes Town meant Carno finished in fifth position in 2011/12 before finding themselves in the lower-half of the table 12 months later. The villagers bounced back in 2013/14 by enjoying a third-placed finish and overcoming Waterloo Rovers 1-0 in the Montgomeryshire Challenge Cup final courtesy of a Peter Rees strike. He would go on to be named player of the season in the Mid Wales League, the first time a Carno player had received that accolade since John Davies, back in the 1990s.

The 2015/16 season was one to remember for everyone connected with the Tŷ Brith club. Carno finished in third position and reached the last-eight stage of the FAW Trophy. The original match with Sully Sports was abandoned after approximately 70 minutes due to a waterlogged pitch before the Montgomeryshire men were defeated 2-0 after extra-time by Sully Sports in the replayed match at Latham Park. Carno also reached the semi-final stage of the League Cup and Radnorshire Cup as well as negotiating their way to the Central Wales Challenge Cup final for the first time. With the match finishing goalless after extra-time, the Greens prevailed 4-3 on penalties to lift the trophy, but were unable to make it a cup double when defeated 3-1 by Llanfair United in the Montgomeryshire Challenge Cup final.

The following term saw Carno enjoy their highest league finish for 16 years after finishing runners-up to Rhayader Town at the summit of the Mid Wales League after a 24-match unbeaten run. The 2017/18 campaign saw manager Chris Davies step down from the helm for three months, replaced by Jonathan Evans and Phil Richards as the Greens concluded the campaign in seventh position. The villagers repeated the feat 12 months later before Davies stood down in the summer of 2019. Several players followed the manager out of the club and Gwynfor Evans took over in an effort to stabilise at the beginning of the 2019/20 season. After nine matches of the campaign, Evans was replaced as manager by Gary Jones, but he was unable to keep his charges from finishing in the lower-half of the table. The campaign was curtailed early due to the Covid pandemic when the final table was determined on a points per game basis.

The Montgomeryshire club were invited to become members of the FAW's new Ardal League for the following term but the competition did not get underway until the 2021/22 season. The debut season in the new competition was not to be a successful one as Carno were relegated at the conclusion of the inaugural campaign before struggling in the lower reaches of the MMP Central Wales League (North) during the following term. Last term saw a slight improvement in fortunes but manager Paul Canning decided to stand down before the current campaign. He was replaced by Callum Breeze and Kieran Beaton and the new management team at Tŷ Brith brought in several new players to strengthen the squad. Carno have made an impressive start to the MMP Central Wales (North) campaign and overcame higher-graded Radnor Valley in the JD Welsh Cup. Having stalled in recent seasons, the club that was born out of a car accident, might be looking to mount a drive back up the pyramid.

Stuart Townsend

Tŷ Brith, pictured left and above, lies directly on the main A470 trunk road, at the north-west end of the village. By public transport, Caersws station is several miles to the east, but the village is served by the T12 bus service which runs along the A470.

Twenty-five years ago, Inter Cardiff were the Welsh Cup holders and had qualified for the UEFA Cup. The draw paired them with Slovenian cup winners NK HIT Gorica, from the town of Nova Gorica on the Italy/Slovenia border.

Inter were not blessed with a large fanbase, and although they'd have some representation from the official party, there wasn't any fans' travel arranged. A few of us from the area, feeling the Welsh Cup winners should have some support in Europe, decided to make our way out to Slovenia independently.

Taking a cheap flight from Stansted, we made our way to Venice by rail, and then on by a local train to the Italian border town of Gorizia, which we'd established was within walking distance of its 'twin' town on the other side of the border. We found a modest hotel on the Italian side.

Slovenia had only been independent from Yugoslavia since 1991, and although the latter had never been technically behind the 'Iron Curtain', the border crossing had been the meeting of western and communist Europe. It still had a certain tension and passports were carefully inspected and stamped each time we ventured across into Slovenia.

12 August 1999, match-day in Nova Gorica, was sweltering. The union jack flag was flying on arrival and was only replaced by a makeshift travelling Welsh one after protests. The open stadium offered little shade from the sun despite a 5pm kick-off and the conditions favoured the home side against Phil Holme's Inter. The tactics seemed to be cautious and defensive, despite his side carrying an attacking threat including Steve Mardenborough. With legendary former Merthyr keeper Gary Wager on the team-sheet, a clean sheet was the target.

For 73 minutes Inter killed the game, restricting the home side to long shots. Then a penalty broke the deadlock and after that Gorica soon doubled the lead, leaving Inter to chase a precious away goal, which didn't materialise. Neither camp seemed very happy after the game – the Slovenian officials bemoaning Inter's negativity and the visitors despondent that the game plan hadn't worked.

Later that night we trekked back over the border, four males on foot crossing into the west – which aroused suspicion as we entered Italy. It took a couple of minutes to persuade armed Italian police that we were football fans, not refugees.

Back in Cardiff, the return leg was played at Cardiff Athletic Stadium – the only UEFA tie staged at the old Leckwith venue. Inter very nearly turned the tie round, Carl Mainwaring's goal with over half an hour left to play put the tie in the balance, but Inter couldn't find a second. The game rather confirmed views formed out in Slovenia that the opposition had been afforded too much respect, as a more positive game plan over two legs might have worked.

D.C.

Below left to right: The single page match programme from HIT Gorica v Inter Cardiff and the local paper report the following morning.

FOLLOWING INTER IN EUROPE

Above: border crossing; match poster; the open main tribune at Gorica.
Below: the teams line up in Gorica, Inter in yellow.

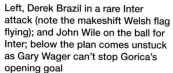

Left, Derek Brazil in a rare Inter attack (note the makeshift Welsh flag flying); and John Wile on the ball for Inter; below the plan comes unstuck as Gary Wager can't stop Gorica's opening goal

THE 1999-2000 SEASON

The summer of 1999 brought the usual round of Welsh action in Europe, and it was all too brief. Aberystwyth Town were up first, competing in the Intertoto Cup. Despite an exciting 2-2 draw in front of their own fans at Park Avenue, the Seasiders lost 4-3 on aggregate to Floriana of Malta.

Barry Town also faced Maltese opposition, in the UEFA Champions League. A 0-0 draw at Jenner Park was disappointing enough, but the 3-2 defeat in Valletta was considered one of the worst in Barry's European adventures.

The Welsh clubs playing in the UEFA Cup that summer were cup winners Inter Cardiff and Cwmbran Town (see the previous two pages for a feature on Inter's tie). Whereas the other three clubs had received apparently favourable draws (but were unable to take advantage) the Crows were handed a money-spinning but impossible task against Celtic. They lost 10-0 on aggregate, much as expected.

And so the new League of Wales season started with plenty of comment about another poor showing in Europe by its representatives. The FAW was known to be concerned, and in 1999 the association's focus seemed to be on trying to find a way of getting a route into Europe for the Anglo clubs, hoping at first to use the FAW Premier Cup competition. When this was rejected, they sounded out UEFA on the question of allowing the exiles back into the Welsh Cup. But UEFA once again reiterated why this was a non-starter.

Writing in Welsh Football's August and September 1999 issues, Alun Evans addressed these issues diplomatically, recognising the problem and also outlining some of the challenges in solving them. The whole debate dominated Alun's two columns in the magazine that summer, and overshadowed the start to the new domestic season. The biggest story within the League of Wales was that champions Barry Town were up for sale. Not just this, but successful manager Gary Barnett departed Jenner Park, to be replaced by Richard Jones for the new campaign. It was certainly the first real sign of setbacks for the dominant Barry club whose progress through previous seasons had been serene. But nobody was writing them off and indeed they started the new season as favourites to retain the title.

The challengers were emerging, nevertheless. Whereas in previous seasons Cwmbran Town and Inter Cardiff were Barry's most likely pursuers, these powers were on the wane and Total Network Solutions now presented as the pretenders to the crown.

In forthcoming issues, we will tell the story of how the 1999-2000 season unfolded.

50 YEARS AGO

The 1974-75 football season began with Cardiff City in Division Two, Wrexham in Division Three, and Newport County and Swansea City in Division Four.

The previous campaign hadn't been anything to write home about, but at least for Cardiff, as Welsh Cup winners, there was a late summer adventure into the European Cup-Winners' Cup. After a poor start to the league campaign, further marred by a riot at Ninian Park during the Second Division game with Manchester United, the Bluebirds flew to Budapest for their First Round, First Leg game with Ferencváros at a low ebb. They were without star Leighton Phillips, who was about to be sold to Aston Villa, and were also missing first choice players Gil Reece, Phil Dwyer and George Smith.

Unsurprisingly, City faced a rearguard action in the Ulloi Stadium on 18 September 1974, and came away with just a 2-0 defeat. For the return leg, two weeks later, only 4,228 spectators paid to watch City attempt to turn the deficit around, the lowest for any first team game since the war. After a goal-less first half, manager Jimmy Andrews gambled by pushing Phil Dwyer into attack. But the gamble didn't pay off, as the Hungarian side scored four times. Phil Dwyer's headed goal meant the aggregate defeat was 6-1, but this was City's worst defeat in ten years of European competition.

Barry Town and Merthyr Tydfil continued to compete in the Southern League and there was a rare highlight for Basil Bright's Linnets in the autumn – the perennial Southern League strugglers ventured into the top half of the league table for the first time in twelve years.

On the international front, Wales were embarking on the qualifying campaign for the 1976 Euros, under the management of Mike Smith. It was now eighteen barren years since Wales had reached the later stages of any competition and hopes weren't helped by an opening 2-1 defeat in Vienna in September 1974. Further qualifying games were to come, both at home, in October and November.

Four south Wales clubs started out in the early stages of the FA Cup, but Barry crashed out in an extra Preliminary Round, followed by Merthyr, Llanelli and Ton Pentre in the First Qualifying Round. In fact, their north Wales counterparts fared better, with Bethesda Athletic beating South Liverpool and Blaenau

Ffestiniog taking Oswestry Town to a replay. Bethesda's Second Qualifying Round tie with Rhyl twice ended 2-2, but the Lilywhites – then a Cheshire League club – eventually won 3-0 in a second replay.

Illustrations left are programme covers from late summer / autumn 1974.

THE 1949-50 SEASON

The 1949-50 season began with both Cardiff City and Swansea Town competing in the Football League Division Two, while Newport County and Wrexham remained in the regionalised Third Divisions.

The South Wales Evening Post's "Football Annual" publication, previewing the 1949-50 season, described a "post war football boom", with huge crowds being recorded in the professional game. In particular, they claimed that "a vast porting public has rejoiced at the return of Swansea Town to the Second Division".

Merthyr Tydfil were flying high in the Southern League, looking to re-capture the league championship after falling short in 1948-49, and Rhyl were hoping to go one better after finishing as runners-up in the Cheshire League. Bangor continued to compete in the Lancashire Combination, with the Welsh Counties Annual reporting that they'd travelled a distance of 5,000 miles in fulfilling the previous season's league fixtures, "a record for a northern non-league club".

In domestic football, Llandudno Junction went into the new season as the defending champions of the Welsh League (North) Division One, and in the south the west Wales trio of Milford United, Haverfordwest Athletic and Llanelli were hoping to topple the strong Merthyr club's reserve string.

The Swansea Evening Post annual also covered local domestic football in some depth. One of its articles claimed, rather controversially, that "West Wales has probably done more to foster soccer than any other area in the Principality" going on to lament the area's lack of representation on the Welsh FA. Elsewhere it reported local football's successful recovery from the Second World War, noting that the Swansea League had "approximately 100 clubs affiliated to it, divided into eight divisions", while in Pembrokeshire, "in addition to the three senior Welsh League clubs, nearly 30 other clubs participated in keen league competition".

32

100 YEARS AGO | 125 YEARS AGO

THE 1924-25 SEASON

The six Welsh clubs in the (English) Football League entered the 1924-25 season with widely differing expectations. Top of the pile were Cardiff City, who had so narrowly missed out on the English title a few months earlier and were hoping to go one better.

Next came Wrexham in the Third Division (North) and Swansea Town, Newport County, Merthyr Town and Aberdare Athletic in the Third Division (South). The economic climate in the south Wales valleys was making life very tough for Aberdare and Merthyr, with the closure of Bedlinog colliery a further blow to employment in the latter's catchment area. Cyfartha colliery followed suit and it was reported that 10,000 miners in the borough were without work by the autumn of 1924. Attendances and gate income at Penydarren Park were falling and the club's fortunes were inevitably impacted.

Over the mountain at Aberdare, things were a little better, despite the economic situation. New seats had been installed in the fire-damaged main stand at the Ynys, and a new manager, Sid Beaumont, had taken charge.

A few Welsh clubs continued in English non-league, with Bridgend Town, Mid Rhondda, Pontypridd, Barry, Ebbw Vale, Aberaman and Llanelly all competing in the Western Section of the Southern League.

The top domestic league in the south, the Welsh League, was heavily dominated by the reserve sides of the Football League and Southern League contingents. By contrast, the lack of cross-border competition in the north meant a more vibrant local league, with Mold, Flint, Holyhead and Rhyl all strong in the Welsh National League (North) of this era.

Plenty of Welsh clubs set out on the FA Cup trail in the autumn of 1924, with the Extra Preliminary Round including Bangor City, Llandudno, Barry, Cardiff Corinthians, Llanelly and Pontypridd. The Football League clubs would join later.

Sources include: Phil Sweet's books on Merthyr Town and Aberdare Athletic.

125 YEARS AGO

THE 1899-1900 SEASON

As the end of the nineteenth century approached, football in Wales was still centred around the north-east of the country. Old rivals Wrexham and Druids had contested the 1899 cup final, and these two, with near neighbours Chirk, continued to lead the small Welsh contingent playing in The Combination, one of the most prominent leagues below the two-division (English) Football League.

The 1899-1900 season began with no Welsh clubs in the Football League, but seven in a reduced complement in The Combination – together with just Oswestry United and Birkenhead. Several Lancashire members had switched to the Lancashire Combination instead. The shift in membership from Merseyside to Wales obviously increased the chance of a first Welsh cross-border triumph (Chirk had come closest, finishing third in 1898).

FA Cup Records show just five clubs based in Wales entering, Aberystwyth, Newtown, Druids, Llandudno Swifts and Wrexham (though you could possibly add Oswestry United and London Welsh to that to make seven 'Welsh' clubs). None of them would get past the qualifying rounds, Wrexham the last standing, but 5-1 losers in the Fourth Qualifying round away to Small Heath, predecessors of Birmingham City.

Domestically, the first incarnation of the North Wales Coast League was still operating, entering its seventh season, while at the other end of the country the South Wales League had now been running for nine years, with clubs like Rogerstone, Treharris, Aberdare and Barry Unionists. Football in South Wales was still amateur, the matter having been the subject of heated debate at the South Wales & Monmouthshire FA AGM in May 1899, the meeting standing firm and voting to continue to outlaw professionalism. It proved to be a pyrrhic victory, for times were changing.

The autumn of 1899 is also significant, in retrospect, for the creation of a new Cardiff club. Bristol-born Bartley Wilson proposed a football section as a way of keeping Riverside Cricket Club members together in the winter months. The club was formed as Riverside FC and records show that it played its first ever fixture on 7 October 1899, a 9–1 defeat to Barry West End. Inauspicious beginnings, but within a quarter of a century they would be at the pinnacle of the English game.

INTERNATIONAL SCENE

While this edition is being printed, Craig Bellamy will be beginning his Cymru managerial career with the first of this autumn's UEFA Nations League (Group B) fixtures against Turkey on September 6 and away to Montenegro three days later.

Ahead of this campaign, Bellamy announced his backroom coaching staff appointments:

Andrew Crofts was appointed as Assistant Coach. Crofts played for various clubs in the English professional game, including Norwich and Brighton, but also had brief spells with Wrexham and Newport. He was capped 29 times for Cymru under John Toshack, Gary Speed and Chris Coleman and completed his UEFA coaching badges through the FAW Coach Education system. Crofts retired from playing in 2019, becoming a coach in Brighton & Hove Albion's academy prior to stepping up as U23s Head Coach in 2021. In 2022, he was appointed First Team Coach under Roberto De Zerbi and Brighton secured European football, reaching the last 16 of the UEFA Europa League last season.

James Rowberry has also been named as an Assistant Coach. Rowberry, whose father Steve played for Newport County in the 1990s, played youth football for Bristol City and Newport, but retired at the age of 21 to concentrate on coaching. He became one of the youngest people to complete his UEFA Pro Licence at the age of 29. He worked at Cardiff City for eight years, initially in the academy setup prior to becoming a First Team Coach under several managers, including Neil Warnock. Following a period as Head Coach of his home-town club Newport County, Rowberry was appointed as the FAW's Head of Elite Coach Education in February 2023, combining the role with coaching in the Cymru junior age group setup.

Another August assistant coach appointment was Ryland Morgans – who was previously involved in Chris Coleman's set up during the Euro 2016 campaign – and Dutchman Piet Cremers, a former colleague of Bellamy's at Burnley.

Craig Bellamy's assistant coaching team is completed by Martyn Margetson, the goalkeeping coach returning to the Cymru set-up, having been involved in the successful 2016 Euros qualification campaign.

Forthcoming matches:

6 Sep Wales v Turkey - Cardiff City Stadium (UEFA Nations League Group B4)

9 Sep Montenegro v Wales - Gradski Stadion, Podgorica (UEFA Nations League Group B4)

11 Oct Iceland v Wales – Laugardalsvöllur, Reykjavík (UEFA Nations League Group B4)

14 Oct Wales v Montenegro - Cardiff City Stadium (UEFA Nations League Group B4)

16 Nov 24 Turkey v Wales (UEFA Nations League Group B4)

19 Nov 24 Wales v Iceland (UEFA Nations League Group B4)

CONTRIBUTORS WANTED

We are always very grateful to receive match photos for use in the magazine.

Thanks to some regular contributors we are able to include a wide variety of action, and special thanks are therefore due to Stuart Townsend (Barcud Coch Protography), all the official FAW Photographers, Steven Jones, Jeff Jones and John Higgins.

But it would be great to receive more, from anyone whether they are regular club photographers, supporters of a Welsh club or groundhoppers. Photos taken on smartphones these days are of good quality and reproduce well, so don't be deterred if you don't use expensive camera equipment.

It would be particularly good to have more photo contributions covering games in the north west of Wales, but the editor would be pleased to hear from anyone, wherever they are based.

Supplement to WF 256
FIXTURES & RESULTS
(compiled 4th September 2024)

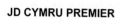

JD CYMRU PREMIER

Phase 1

	P	W	D	L	F	A	Pt
Penybont	5	3	2	0	9	2	11
Cardiff Met Univ.	5	3	2	0	10	4	11
Haverfordwest C.	5	3	2	0	6	1	11
Bala Town	5	2	2	1	6	3	8
Connahs Quay N	5	2	1	1	7	3	7
Newtown	5	2	1	2	6	9	7
The New Saints	2	2	0	0	6	1	6
Barry Town Utd	5	1	2	2	6	7	5
Caernarfon Tn.	4	1	1	2	6	4	4
Aberystwyth Tn.	5	1	1	3	4	12	4
Flint Town Utd	5	0	0	5	4	12	0
Briton Ferry Ll.	5	0	0	5	2	14	0

Phase 1 consists of 22 rounds of fixtures after which the league splits into two groups of six for the second phase.

JD CYMRU NORTH

	P	W	D	L	F	A	Pt
Airbus UK	6	6	0	0	22	2	18
Holywell Town	6	4	0	2	17	9	12
Bangor 1876	6	4	0	2	14	8	12
Colwyn Bay	6	3	2	1	7	7	11
Buckley Town	5	3	1	1	8	3	10
Mold Alexandra	6	3	0	3	14	9	9
Guilsfield	5	3	0	2	12	7	9
Flint Mountain	6	3	0	3	14	10	9
Caersws	5	3	0	2	8	9	9
Penrhyncoch	5	2	1	2	9	11	7
Ruthin Town	6	2	0	4	16	18	6
Denbigh Town	5	2	0	3	10	14	6
Llandudno	6	1	1	4	6	13	4
Gresford Athletic	6	1	1	4	6	15	4
Prestatyn Town	5	1	0	4	5	24	3
Llay Welfare	6	0	2	4	7	16	2

JD CYMRU SOUTH

	P	W	D	L	F	A	Pt
Trethomas Blueb..	6	4	2	0	14	6	14
Trefelin BGC	6	4	1	1	13	7	13
Carmarthen Town	6	3	2	1	14	10	11
Newport City	6	3	2	1	8	5	11
Cambrian United	6	3	2	1	8	6	11
Llanelli Town	6	2	4	0	12	7	10
Llantwit Major	6	3	1	2	12	9	10
Goytre United	6	3	1	2	12	10	10
Pontypridd United	6	3	1	2	11	13	10
Taffs Well	6	2	1	3	6	13	7
Cwmbran Celtic	6	2	0	4	9	11	6
Caerau Ely	6	1	2	3	8	8	5
Afan Lido	6	1	2	3	9	10	5
Baglan Dragons	6	1	2	3	5	9	5
Ammanford	6	1	0	5	8	15	3
Penrhiceiber R.	6	0	1	5	2	12	1

ARDAL LEAGUES

Lock Stock ARDAL NE

	P	W	D	L	F	A	Pt
Brickfield Rangers	5	5	0	0	18	9	15
Bow Street	6	4	1	1	14	3	13
Llangollen Town	5	4	0	1	17	10	12
Kerry	6	4	0	2	17	11	12
Builth Wells	6	3	2	1	19	8	11
Cefn Albion	5	3	1	1	16	7	10
Penycae	5	3	0	2	12	9	9
Llanuwchllyn	5	3	0	2	9	8	9
Dolgellau AA	4	2	1	1	10	9	7
Llanfair United	4	2	0	2	8	5	6
Llandrindod Wells	5	1	1	3	7	12	4
Radnor Valley	6	1	1	4	13	19	4
Llanidloes Town	6	1	1	4	12	20	4
Rhos Aelwyd	5	1	0	4	5	12	3
Llansantffraid V.	5	1	0	4	5	21	3
Chirk AAA	6	0	0	6	3	22	0

Lock Stock ARDAL NW

	P	W	D	L	F	A	Pt
Porthmadog	5	4	1	0	17	6	13
Connahs Quay Tn.	5	4	1	0	13	8	13
Y Rhyl 1879	5	4	0	1	11	5	12
Llangefni Town	5	3	1	1	10	4	10
Holyhead Hotspur	5	3	1	1	8	4	10
NFA	5	3	0	2	7	10	9
Llanrwst United	5	2	2	1	10	8	8
Trearddur Bay	5	2	2	1	5	4	8
Pwllheli	5	1	2	2	7	7	5
Corwen	5	1	2	2	11	13	5
Llannefydd	5	1	1	3	7	9	4
St Asaph City	5	1	1	3	1	4	4
Nantlle Vale	5	1	1	3	5	9	4
Y Felinheli	5	1	1	3	6	11	4
Conwy Borough	5	1	0	4	6	13	3
Menai Br. Tigers	5	0	0	5	5	14	0

Floodlighting & Electrical ARDAL SE

	P	W	D	L	F	A	Pt
Treowen Stars	6	5	0	1	18	4	15
Canton FC	7	4	2	1	9	5	14
Brecon Corries	5	4	1	0	13	3	13
Aber. Bluebirds	7	4	1	2	22	14	13
Chepstow Town	6	4	0	2	21	5	12
Abergavenny Tn	6	3	3	0	10	4	12
Abercarn United	5	2	2	1	8	9	8
Goytre AFC	5	2	1	2	8	8	7
Caldicot Town	5	2	1	2	6	11	7
Blaenavon Blues	6	2	0	4	6	11	6
Newport Corries	5	1	2	2	6	9	5
Croesyceiliog	6	1	1	4	12	14	4
Risca United	5	1	1	3	8	18	4
Undy	6	1	1	4	9	24	4
Treharris Ath W.	5	1	0	4	3	10	3
Tredegar Town	5	0	0	5	5	15	0

Floodlighting & Electrical ARDAL SW

	P	W	D	L	F	A	Pt
Cefn Cribwr	6	4	1	1	10	4	13
Evans & Williams	6	4	1	1	10	7	13
Cardiff Corries	5	3	2	0	18	7	11
Cardiff Draconians	5	3	2	0	11	4	11
Ynyshir Albions	5	2	2	1	4	3	8
Treherbert BGC	5	1	3	1	5	4	6
South Gower	4	2	0	2	6	6	6
Morriston Town	4	2	0	2	3	4	6
Swansea Univ.	5	2	0	3	7	10	6
Clydach FC	5	1	2	2	7	8	5
Pontardawe Town	6	1	2	3	6	7	5
Ynysygerwn	5	1	2	2	6	9	5
AFC Llwydcoed	4	1	1	2	6	8	4
Seven S. Onllwyn	5	0	3	2	6	10	3
Bridgend Street	4	1	0	3	5	12	3
Pontyclun	6	0	3	3	4	11	3

UEFA CLUB COMPETITIONS:

UEFA CHAMPIONS LEAGUE
2nd Qualifying Round
Ferencváros - TNS 5-0
TNS – Ferencváros 1-2 (agg 1-7)

UEFA EUROPA LEAGUE
3rd Qualifying Round
Petrocub – TNS 1-0
TNS – Petrocub 0-0 (agg 0-1)

UEFA CONFERENCE LEAGUE
2nd Qualifying Round
Legia Warszawa - Caernarfon Town 6-0
Caernarfon Town v Legia Warszawa 0-5
(agg 0-11)

UEFA CONFERENCE LEAGUE –
Play Off Round
Panevėžys – TNS 0-3
TNS – Panevėžys 0-0 (agg 3-0)

UEFA CONFERENCE LEAGUE
GROUP STAGE FIXTURES

03 Oct: Fiorentina v TNS

24 Oct: TNS v FC Astana

07 Nov: Shamrock Rovers v TNS

28 Nov: TNS v Djurgårdens

12 Dec: TNS v Panthinaikos

19 Dec: NK Celje v TNS

Venues to be announced

DOMESTIC CUP COMPETITIONS

(r) = tie reversed, disq. = disqualified, w/d = withdrew, w/o = walk over, AET = after extra time

NATHANIEL MG CUP Round 2 (South) Briton Ferry Llansawel - Penybont 0-3, Cardiff City - Pontypridd United 3-1, Trethomas Bluebirds - Baglan Dragons 3-1, Carmarthen Town - Haverfordwest County 0-5, Merthyr Town – Ammanford 2-0, Goytre United - Caerau Ely 3-2, Llantwit Major - Cardiff Met 2-3, Barry Town United - Llanelli Town 1-1 5-3 pens. **(North)** Buckley Town – Connah's Quay Nomads 0-3, The New Saints - Flint Town United 5-1, Llandudno - Guilsfield 2-2 4-2 pens, Gresford Athletic - Airbus UK Broughton 1-4, Ruthin Town - Bala Town 0-1, Colwyn Bay - Aberystwyth T. 0-2, Newtown - Caernarfon T. 2-2 1-3 pens, Holywell Town - Llay Welfare 3 -1
Round 3 (17-18 September): Aberystwyth Town v Llandudno, Airbus UK v The New Saints, Bala Town v Holywell Town, Cardiff City v Merthyr Town, Cardiff Met Uni v Goytre Utd, Connah's Quay Nomads v Caernarfon Town, Penybont v Haverfordwest Co., Trethomas Bluebirds v Barry Town Utd.
Quarter-Finals: 22-23 October, Semi-Finals: 28-30 November, Final: 28 February-2 March 2025

Welsh Blood Service **LEAGUE CUP Round 1: Northern section:** Airbus UK Broughton – Llandudno 3-1, Buckley Town - Llay Welfare 1-2, Caersws - Bangor 1876 1-1 3-5 pens, Flint Mountain - Colwyn Bay 1-1 3-4 pens, Gresford Ath - Denbigh T. 3-0, Mold Alex - Holywell Town 0-1, Penrhyncoch - Prestatyn T. 1-0, Ruthin T. – Guilsfield 3-0. **Southern section:** Afan Lido - Carmarthen T. 0-1, Ammanford - Llantwit Major 1-1 2-0 pens, Cwmbran Celtic - Taffs Well 2-3, Goytre Utd - Pontypridd Utd 1-2, Newport City - Llanelli T. 1-1 4-2 pens, Penrhiwceiber R. - Baglan Dragons 4-3, Trefelin - Cambrian Utd 3-1, Trethomas Bluebirds - Caerau Ely 0-1 **Round 2:** 31.1-2.2.25: **(N)** Bangor 1876 v Ruthin T., Gresford Ath v Colwyn Bay, Llay Welfare v Airbus UK, Penrhyncoch v Holywell Town. **(S)** Caerau Ely v Pontypridd Utd, Newport City v Ammanford, Penrhiwceiber R v Carmarthen T., Trefelin v Taffs Well.

JD WELSH CUP Second Qualifying Round: (South) Aberdare Town - Newport Corinthians 0-1, Abertillery Bluebirds - Cascade YC 3-2, AFC Llwydcoed - Croesceiliog 4-2, Blaenavon Blues - Cardiff Corinthians 1-4, Bryn Rovers - Chepstow Town 3-5, Builth Wells - Cefn Cribwr 3-0, Cardiff Bay Warriors - Cwrt Rawlin 7-3, Cardiff Dracs - Bettws 4-0, Clwb Cymric - Cwm Wdrs 2-1, Clydach FC - West End 2-2 1-3 pens, Cwmbran Town - Llangeinor 3-0, Ely Rangers - Treforest 5-2, FC Cwmaman - Cwmamman Utd 1-2, Ffostrasol - Pencoed Ath 1-2, Goytre – Pontyclun 1-1 4-2 pens, Holton Road - Pill 3-6, Monmouth T. - Seven Sisters Onllwyn 1-1 5-4 pens, Morriston Town - Port Talbot T. 1-0, New Inn - Evans & Williams 3-2, Penlan - Caldicot Town 2-2 5-6 pens, Penydarren BGC - Canton 5-0 (Abandoned), Pontardawe Town - Aber Valley 3-4, Porthcawl Town - Newport Saints 4-1, Risca Utd - Seaside 3-0, Rogerstone - Dafen Welfare 5-1, St Josephs - AFC Bargoed 13-0, Swansea Univ. - Caerphilly Ath 1-1 6-5 pens, Treherbert BGC - Pantyscallog Village 3-2, Ynysygerwn - Cardiff Airport 4-3.
(North) Amlwch Town - Porthmadog 0-5, Bro Cernyw - Llandudno Amateurs 0-3, Carno - Penycae 2-1, Cefn Albion - Penrhyndeudraeth 6-3, Cerrigydrudion - Llansantffraid V 3-1, Cemaes Bay - Llanrwst United 0-3, Connah's Quay Town - Brickfield Rangers 2-4, FC Queens Park - Blaenau Ffestiniog Amateurs 3-1, Holyhead Hotspur - Bethesda Ath 4-2, Kinmel Bay - Bow 3-2, Llanberis - Bontnewydd 4-1, Llangefni Town - Chirk AAA (r) 7-3, Llangollen Town - Y Felinheli 2-0, Llannefydd - Penyffordd Lions 4-2, Llanrhaeadr - Llanystumdwy 3-1, Llansannan - Conwy Boro 2-2 5-4 pens, Llanuwchllyn - Berriew 10-0, Montgomery T. - Corwen (r) 1-4, Nefyn Utd - Menai Bridge Tigers 3-3 2-4 pens, NFA - Henllan 3-1, Penmaenmawr Phoenix - Pwllheli 5-2, Rhostyllen - St Asaph C. 2-3, Rhos Aelwyd - Gaerwen 0-2, Rhydymwyn - Boded 3-1, Y Rhyl 1879 - Glan Conwy 6-0, Talysarn Celts - Llandrindod Wells 1-0, Trearddur Bay - Llanfairfechan Town 7-0.

Round 1 (20th-21st September) **South:** Aber Valley v Cwmamman United, Caldicot Town v Morriston Town, Cardiff Bay Warriors v West End, Cardiff Corries v Risca United, Chepstow Town v Pill, Cwmbran Celtic v Trefelin BGC, Goytre v Pencoed Athletic, Llantwit Major v Ely Rangers, New Inn v Abertillery Bluebirds, Newport City v Monmouth Town , Newport Corries v AFC Llwydcoed, Penrhiwceiber Rangers v Cwmbran Town, Penydarren or Canton v Porthcawl Town, St. Joseph's v Cardiff Draconians, Swansea University v Baglan Dragons, Taffs Well v Trethomas Bluebirds, Treherbert BGC v Clwb Cymric, Ynysygerwn v Rogerstone.
North: Buckley Town v Builth Wells, Caersws v Cefn Albion, Carno v Llanrhaeadr, Corwen v Llay Welfare, FC Queens Park v Porthmadog, Gresford Athletic v Prestatyn Town, Kinmel Bay v Brickfield Rangers, Llandudno v Llanberis, Llandudno Amateurs v Holyhead Hotspur, Llangefni Town v Gaerwen, Llannefydd v Rhydymwyn, Llanrwst Utd v Menai Bridge Tigers, Llansannan v Cerrigydrudion, Penmaenmawr Phoenix v Llanuwchllyn, Penrhyncoch v Talysarn Celts, St Asaph C. v Llangollen Town, Trearddur Bay v NFA, Y Rhyl 1879 v Flint Mountain

Round 2: 18-19 Oct, Round 3: 15-16 Nov, Round 4: 13-14 Dec, Round 5 (QF) 14-15 Feb '25, Semi-finals 14-15 March, Final: 4 May.

DRAGON SIGNS FAW AMATEUR TROPHY Qualifying Round: SE : Abercarn Utd - Ponthir 7-2, Abergavenny Town - Tredegar T. 2-1, AFC Pontymister - Aber Excelsiors 4-1, Albion Rovers - Machen 3-1, , Bettws - Brynmawr Utd 5-0, Clydach Wasps - Newport Saints 2-2 5-3 pens, Cwmbach RS - Undy 3-3 4-2 pens, Cwmcarn Ath - AFC Wattstown 1-3, Goytre AFC - Rogerstone 3-3 5-4 pens, Lliswerry - Bridgend Street 2-2 8-9 pens, Mardy w/o Underwood, Nantyglo - Brecon Corries 4-2, Newbridge Town - Coed Eva Ath. 3-2, Newport Corries w/o Panteg, Pentwynmawr - Monmouth T. (r) 2-2 5-3 pens, Portskewett & S. - Nelson Cavaliers 2-9, Risca United - New Inn 6-1, Riverside Rovers - Treowen Stars 0-6, Thornwell - Alway (r) 8-4, Twyn y Ffaldd Blues - Graig Villa Dino 1-6
SOUTH CENTRAL : Aber Valley - Caerphilly Ath 3-0, Aberfan Rgs - Canton 0-8, AFC Llwydcoed - Canton Rgs 9-1, AFC Penrhiwceiber - Vale Utd 2-0, Brynna - Treharris Ath 0-2, Cardiff Airport - Clwb Cymric 2-2 7-6 pens, Cardiff Bay - AFC Bargoed 3-5, Cardiff Bay Warriors - Aberdare Town 3-4, Cardiff Corries - The Baglan 3-0, Cardiff Dracs - Tonyrefail BGC 1-0, Clwb Sparta - Dinas Powys 0-1, Cogan - Maesteg Pk 8-0, Cwrt y Vil - Heolgerrig Red Lion 0-2, Ely Rangers - Pantyscallog V (r) 3-3 4-3 pens, FC Cwmaman w/o Penrhiwceiber Navigation, Grange Albion - Pencoed Ath 1-2, Llandaff Cosmos - Holton Road 2-8, Llangeinor - Ely Valley (r) 7-0,

2

Llanrumney Utd - Carn Rovers 3-0, Penygraig BGC - Penygraig Utd 1-9, Rhydyfelin - Cwrt Rawlin 4-1, Splott Cons - Margam YC 4-3, Sully Sp - AFC Whitchurch, Tiger Bay – Treforest 1-4, Ton Pentre - Radyr Rangers 5-0, Tongwynlais – Llanishen FC 2-3, Tonyrefail Welfare - Penydarren BGC 0-8, Treherbert BGC - Barry Athletic (r) 1-0, Ynyshir Albions - Black Lion 7-0

SW: Birchgrove Colts - Ragged School 3-2, Blaenymaes – Swansea Univ. 3-2, Bryn Rovers - Bonymaen Colts 3-0, Cilfrew Rovers - Llangennech 3-4, CKSV - St Josephs (Swansea) 0-8, Clase Social - Dafen Welfare 1-7, FC Bonymaen - Port Talbot Town 1-4, Garw - Ynysygerwn 0-6, Giants Grave - Bryncoch 1-0, Glyncorrwg - South Gower 1-3, Llandarcy - Cwm Wanderers 3-1, Merlins Bridge - Ynystawe Ath 1-5, Morriston Town - Porthcawl Town 1-1 5-4 pens, Mumbles Rangers - Clydach FC 1-0, Penlan - Garden Village 1-1 5-4 pens, Pontarddulais T. - Port Tennant Colts 7-1, Rockspur - Neath Town 7-1, Seaside - Penclawdd 10-2, Seven Sisters Onllwyn - Tata Steel Utd 1-1 2-4 pens, West End - Glynneath Town 3-0.

CENTRAL: Berriew - Llanilar 1-0, Bow Street - Tregaron Turfs 7-0, Dyffryn Banw - Radnor Valley 1-3, Four Crosses - Machynlleth 1-1 4-2 pens, Hay St Mary's - Trewern Utd 0-4, Llandrindod Wells - Montgomery Town 2-3, Llanrhaeadr - Llansantffraid Village 7-0, Kerry - Penybont Utd (r) 12-0, Tywyn Bryncrug - Barmouth & D. 4-2, Waterloo Rovers - Llanfair Utd 2-0, Welshpool Town - Dolgellau AA

NE: Brickfield Rgs - Henllan 7-1, Bro Cernyw - Bow 1-7, Caerwys - Llandyrnnog U. 0-1, Cefn Albion - St Asaph City 2-1, Cei Connah w/d v Corwen w/o, Cerrigydrudion - Rhos Aelwyd 2-1, Connahs Quay Town - Greenfield 5-1, Deesside Dragons - Rhuddlan T 2-2 4-5 pens, FC Queens Pk - Rhydymwyn 2-2 5-4 pens, Gronant - Rhyl Albion 2-1, Holywell Utd - Coedpoeth U. 0-3, Kinmel Bay - Penycae 2-1, Llangollen Town - Y Glannnau 1-0, Llannefydd - Prestatyn Sports 8-0, Mynydd Isa – Meliden 1-1 5-4 pens, Overton Rec - Castell Alun 0-0 4-1 pens, Penyffordd Lions - Acton 0-1, Rhostyllen - Lex XI 1-2, Rhyl 1879 - Llysfaen 9-1, Ruabon Rovers - Llansannan 1-4, Saltney Town - Plas Madoc 2-4

NW: Bethesda Rovers - Llandudno Junction 3-3 4-3 pens, Blaenau Ffestiniog - Bethesda Ath. 2-3, Boded - Llangefni Town 1-0, Cefni - Glantraeth 3-1, Cemaes Bay - NFA 5-1, Conwy Borough - Llandudno Swifts (r) 3-1, Gaerwen - Llanberis 1-2, Gwalchmai - Penrhyndeudraeth 3-2, Holyhead Town - Pentraeth 1-2, Llandudno Amateurs - Pwllheli 2-4, Llanfairfechan Town - Mountain Rangers 5-2, Llangoed & D - Valley 3-0, Llanrug United - Nefyn United 2-2 4-2 pens, Llanystumdwy - Menai Br. Tigers 3-3 5-3 pens, Mochdre Sports - Bontnewydd 1-1 5-4 pens, Nantlle Vale - Amlwch Tn 5-1, Penmaenmawr Ph. - Llanfairpwll 8-1, Rhos United - Llanrwst United 1-2, Talysarn Celts - Holyhead Hotspur 1-4, Trearddur Bay - Caergybi (r) 5-0, Y Felinheli - Llanuwchllyn 2-3.

Round 1: SE Abertillery Bluebirds – Thornwell, AFC Pontymister – Treowen Stars, Albion Rovers – AFC Wattstown, Bettws v Risca Utd (r), Bridgend Street – Llanrumney United, Cwmbach RS – Newport Corinthians, Graig Villa Dino – Abergavenny Town, Mardy – Abercarn Utd, Nelson Cavaliers – Goytre AFC, Newbridge Town – Nantyglo, Pentwynmawr – Clydach Wasps. **S CENTRAL**: Aber Valley – AFC Llwydcoed, AFC Bargoed – Treforest, AFC Penrhiwceiber – Ely Rangers, Cardiff Corries – Rhydyfelin, Cardiff Draconians – Ton Pentre, Heolgerrig – Canton FC, Holton Road – Sully Sports, Llangeinor – Aberdare T., Llanishen – FC Cwmaman, Penygraig Utd – Cardiff Airport, Penydarren BGC – Treherbert BGC, Splott Con – Dinas Powys, Treharris – Cogan Cor. **SW**: Bryn Rovers – Ynystawe Ath, Cefn Cribwr – Ynysygerwn, Giants Grave – Dafen Welfare, Llangennech – Pontarddulais T., Mumbles Rangers – St Josephs, Pontardawe T. – Blaenymaes, Port Talbot Tn – Birchgrove Colts, Seaside – Penlan, South Gower – Rockspur, Tata Steel Utd – Morriston T., West End – Llandarcy.
CENTRAL: Berriew – Montgomery T., Bow Street – Radnor Valley, Four Crosses – Trewern U., Llanrhaeadr – Dolgellau, Llanidloes T. – Kerry, Tywyn Bryncrug – Waterloo Rovers. **NE**: Brickfield R – Llangollen, Cefn Albion – Gronant, Chirk AAA – Mynydd Isa, FC Queens Park – Connahs Quay Town, KInmel Bay – Rhuddlan T., Llandyrnog Utd – Cerrigydrudion, LLannefydd – Corwen, Llansannan – Bow, Overton – Lex XI, Plas Madoc – Acton, Rhyl 1879 – Coedpoeth U, **NW**: Boded – Llanuwchllyn, Cefni – Llanfairfechan , Conwy Bor – Nantlle Vale, Llangoed – Pwllheli, Llanrwst U – Cemaes Bay, Llanystumdwy – Llanberis, Mochdre Sp. – Bethesda Rov, Penmaenmawr – Llanrug U, Pentraeth – Bethesda A., Porthmadog – Holyhead H, Trearddur Bay – Gwalchmai.

ARDAL SOUTHERN LEAGUE CUP Round 1: Caldicot Town – Goytre 3-1, Canton FC - Cardiff Draconians 2-0, Cardiff Corinthians - Blaenavon Blues 2-1, Cefn Cribwr - Seven Sisters Onllwyn 3-0, Chepstow Town - Abergavenny Town 2-2 5-4 pens, Clydach FC - Pontardawe Town 0-2, Evans & Williams – Undy 4-0, Newport Corinthians - Swansea University 3-3 3-5 pens, Pontyclun - Morriston Town 5-1, South Gower - Risca United 3-3 5-3 pens, Tredegar Town - Abercarn United 2-1, Treherbert BGC – Croesyceiliog 5-2, Treharris Athletic Western - Brecon Corries 0-6, Treowen Stars - AFC Llwydcoed 0-3, Ynyshir Albions - Bridgend Street 2-1, Ynysygerwn - Abertillery Bluebirds 1-5

ARDAL NORTHERN LEAGUE CUP Round 1 Bow St. - Llandrindod Wells 4-2, Brickfield Rgs - Llanfair Utd 3-3 5-4 pens, Builth Wells – Kerry 1-1 3-4 pens, Corwen - Holyhead Hotspur 0-0 abandoned, CPD Llannefydd - Conwy Boro 7-1, CPD Y Felinheli - Connah's Quay Town 3-1, CPD Rhyl 1879 – Porthmadog 1-1 5-6 pens, Llangefni Town - Llanrwst Utd 0-0 4-5 pens, Llangollen T. - Cefn Alb. 6-4, Llanidloes T. – Penycae 1-1 3-1 pens, Llansantfraid Village - Rhos Aelwyd 2-1, Llanuwchllyn - Chirk AAA 5-0, Nantlle Vale - St Asaph City 3-1, NFA – Pwllheli 5-0, Radnor Valley - Dolgellau AA 2-1, Trearddur Bay - Menai Bridge Tigers 5-1

Hugh James **SOUTH WALES FA SENIOR CUP – Round 1:** (14 Sep) Aberdare T. v Caerphilly Ath, AFC Abercynon v Llangeinor, AFC Bargoed v Fairwater, Barry Ath v Maesteg Pk, Black Lion v Penrhiwfer, Brecon FC v Cardiff Bay, Caerau All Whites v Pentyrch Rgs, Caerau Ely Community v Gilfach, Canton Rgs v Llwynypia BGC, Cardiff Hibs v Gurnos, Cascade YC v Penygraig BGC, Cathays Cons v Cardiff Academicals, Church Village v Garw, Clwb Sparta v Llangynwyd Rgs, Cwmafan v Bettws, Cwrt Rawlin v AFC Penrhiwceiber, Cwrt-y-Vil v Splott Albion, Dinas Powys v Holton Rd, Glyncorrwg v Llanishen Wdrs, Hopkinstown v Vale Utd, Llanbradach v Margam YC, Llanishen v Pontypridd FC, Merthyr Saints v Aber Exiles, Pantyscallog V v St Athan, Penrhiwceiber Soc. V Bryntirion Ath, Pentwyn D v Ferndale BGC, Penydarren BGC v Cogan, Penyfai v The Baglan, Penygraig U v Llanrumney Ath, Penywaun v Pencoed, Porthcawl T. v Banog, Red Valley v Gwynfi U, Rhoose S. V Thornhill, Talbot Gr v Brynna, Tonyrefail Welfare v Cwm Talwg.

3

Highadmit Projects **SOUTH WALES PREMIER LEAGUE – W. JOHN OWEN CUP.** Preliminary Round: AFC Penrhiwceiber v Tongwynlais, Bettws v Margam YC, Caerphilly Athletic v Dinas Powys, Cardiff Airport v Clwb Cymric, Cardiff Bay Warriors v Tonyrefail BGC, Grange Albion v Port Talbot Town, Llangeinor v Fairwater, Llantwit Fardre v Cwmbach RS, Maesteg Park v Penydarren BGC, Pantyscallog v Caerau All Whites, Pencoed Athletic BGC v Treforest, Penrhiwfer v Nelson Cavaliers, Porthcawl Town v Afan United, Splott Cons v AFC Wattstown, Tata Steel United v Cogan Coronation, Ton Pentre v St Josephs

Macron **WEST WALES PEMIER LEAGUE CUP: First Round:** AFC Glais v Seaside, Bryn Rovers v Mumbles Rangers, CKSV v Cwm Wanderers, Garden Village v Giants Grave, Penlan v Ynystawe Athletic, Pontarddulais Town v Cwmamman Utd, Rockspur v Dafen Welfare, West End v St Joseph's. (Ties to be played 11th/12th October)

WEST WALES FA INTERMEDIATE CUP Rd 1 (5 Oct) AFC Pontardawe v Abergwili, Banffosfelen v Rhos, Birchgrove Colts v Ynysmeudwy, Bonymaen Colts v Kingsbridge Colts, Camford Sp v Ystradgynlais, Camrose v Caerbryn, Carew v Fforestfach, Clase Soc v Monkton S., Coed Darcy v Drefach, Cwm Albion v Harp Rovers, Cwrt Herbert v Brynawel, FC Bonymaen v Clydach Sp, Fishguard Sp v Bwlch Rgs, Gors v Skewen, Johnston v Loughor Rovers, Kidwelly v Talycopa, Killay v Milford Utd, Letterston v Lawrenny, Llandarcy v Ferryside, Llangyfelach v Pengelli U, Merlins Br. V Pembrey, Narberth v Treboeth, Newport Tigers v Plough C., Neyland v Cwmfelin Press, Pennar R v KRUF, Prendergast V v Tumble, Pwll v Cimla, Ragged Sch v Solva, Resolven v Milford Ath, Rosehill v Gorseinon, St Clears v Tonna, St Ishmaels v Hundleton, St Thomas Stars v Murton R, Tenby v Maltsters, Trallwm v Burry Port, Trostre v Cilfrew, West End Utd v Kilgetty

NORTH EAST WALES FA CHALLENGE CUP Qual Round: Acton – Hawarden Rgs 1-6, Broughton Utd – Aston Pk Rangers 4-1, Coedpoeth U – Rhostyllen 0-1, Gronant – Mynydd Isa 1-4, Holywell Utd – Caerwys 6-0, Penyffordd Lions – FC Queens Pk 0-3, Saltney Town – Greenfield 0-2, Ruabon Rovers – Lex XI 1-5, Skippy – Castell Alun 2-11, Yr Wyddgrug – Rhydymwyn 4-4 4-5 pens, **Round 1:** Broughton Utd – Mynydd Isa 4-1, Castell Alun – Hawarden Rgs 1-3, Greenfield – Lex XI 2-3, FC Queens Park – Rhydymwyn 4-0, Rhostyllen – Holywell Utd 4-1.
Round 2: (10 Sep) Airbus UK v Hawarden Rangers, Broughton Utd v Buckley Town, Corwen v Brickfield Rgs, Flint Town Utd v FC Queens Park, Lex XI v Rhostllen, Llay Welfare v Holywell Town, Mold Alex v Flint Mountain, Ruthin Town v Gresford Ath.

NWCFA INTERMEDIATE CUP Rd 1: Boded – Llanystumdwy 4-1, Bontnewydd – Bro Cernyw 4-0, Bow - Llanrug Utd 6-0, Cemaes Bay – Nefyn Utd 4-1, Glan Conwy – Glantraeth 2-3, Kinmel Bay – Meliden 2-1, Llanerchymedd – Bethesda Ath 0-4, Llanfairfechan – M. Llandegai 4-2, Llansannan – Gwalchmai 3-5, Mochdre – Talysarn Celts 0-1, Penmaenmawr – Cerrigydrudion 5-0, Pentraeth – Aberffraw 3-1, Penrhyndeudraeth – Llanberis 2-0, Rhuddlan – Llandyrnog Utd 7-4 aet, Y Glannau – Llandudno Am. 1-2 aet

NWCFA JUNIOR CUP Rd 1: (14/09) Llandudno Swifts v Deiniolen, Rhos United v CPD Cefni, Rhyl Albion v Blaenau Ffestiniog.

CWFA SENIOR CUP: RD 1: Carno – Tregaron 2-1 **RD 2:** Maesglas - Llanfair Utd 0-6, Llandrindod W v Guilsfield, Llanidloes v Four Crosses, Newtown Dev v Builth Wells, Caersws v Llanrhaeadr, Berriew v Kerry, Ffostrasol v Hay St. Mary's, Abermule v Bishops Castle, Llanilar v Machynlleth, Presteigne v Felinfach, Borth Utd v Tywyn Bryncrug, Dyffryn Banw v Welshpool T., Waterloo R v Montgomery, Forden v Penrhyncoch, Bont v Radnor Valley, Carno v Llansantffraid V.

CWFA J EMRYS MORGAN CUP Rd 1: Forden – Llanidloes Res 10-0, St Dogmaels v Aberaeron, Aberporth v Llanboidy. **Rd 2:** Aber Uni v Berriew, Bargod Rangers v Llandrindod Res, Bont v Lampeter, Bishops Castle v Llangedwyn, Bow St Res v Welshpool, Carno v Llanfechain, Caersws Dev v Llanfyllin, Cardigan v Maesglas, Crymych v Llanon, D Banw v Barmouth, Dolgellau Res v Abermule, Ffostrasol v Dewi Stars, Hay St M v Felinfach, Llanilar v Llechryd, Llanfair U Res v Corris U, Llanrhaeadr Res v Montgomery, Meifod v Padarn, New Quay v Felindre, Pencader v Builth Wells Res, Penparcau v Borth U, Penybont Utd v Knighton, Presteigne v Newcastle Emlyn, Rhayader Town v Brecon FC, Talgarth Town v Newcastle, Talybont v Waterloo R, Trefonen v Penrhyncoch Res, Tregaron Turfs v Crannog, Trewern Utd v Kerry Res

N. WALES COAST LEAGUE (E) COOKSON CUP Rd 1 (14/09): Cerrigydrudion v Bro Cernyw, Kinmel Bay v Glan Conwy, Llansannan v Llandyrnog, Llandudno Jct v Llanfairfechan, Mochdre v Llandudno Am., Penmaenmawr v Meliden, Rhuddlan v Y Glannau

Bute Energy **FAW WOMEN'S CUP: First Qualifying Round** (22nd September) Wattsville v Penydarren
2nd Qual. Round: (S) Abertillery Belles v Penclawdd, AFC Llwydcoed v Swansea Univ., Caldicot Town v North Cardiff Cosmos, Cardiff Wdrs v Drefach, Carmarthen T. v Trefelin BGC, Croesyceiliog v Cascade, Johnstown v Aberystwyth Uni, Llanelli T v Morriston T. Llantwit Fardre v Cambrian Utd, Mumbles Rangers v Cwmbran Celtic, Pontarddulais T. v Taffs Well, Pontypridd Utd v Ammanford, Rogerstone v Penybont, Talycopa v Aberaman. Wattsville or Penydarren v Newport City
(N) Airbus v Caernarfon T., Amlwch v Y Rhyl 1879, Bangor v Llandudno, Denbigh v Pwllheli, Kinmel Bay v Y Felinheli, Llanfair Utd v Connahs Quay Nomads, Llangefni T. v Flint Town Utd, Llanystumdwy v Northop Hall, NFA v Berriew.

GENERO ADRAN TROPHY: Group stage matchday 1: Sunday 1 September, Group stage matchday 2: Sunday 8 September, Group stage matchday 3: Sunday 13 October, Round of 16: Sunday 10 November, Quarter-finals: Sunday 8 December, Semi-finals: Sunday 12 January 2025, Final: Sunday 9 February 2025

MORE IN NEXT ISSUE! The next issue, WF 257, will include a double-size supplement (8 pages) with tables down to tier 6.